Your Choice, Your Voice, Our Future

An economic future for the State of Maine

Richard Lee Light

2017

Dedication

This book is in dedication to my son Gabriel Lucien Light and your generation.

Your future depends on our choices today.

Table of Contents

Table of Contents	2
Preface – The Wrong Enemies	4
Civil War - We Are 2 Maines	4
Left and Right - A False Choice	4
Own or Rent?	5
Prologue – Stopping	8
Anarchist Frenemies	10
Separate, Unequal, and Free	10
Moving the Needle	11
Chapter 1 – A Game of Thrones	13
A Governor's Job	16
Overview	16
Approval of State Budgets and Appropriations	17
Enactment of Legislation	17
Gubernatorial Appointments	17
Boards and Commissions	18
My Goals as Governor	19
Chapter 2 – Fiat Economics: A Beginner's Guide	20
Fiat Economics 101: What Is Money?	20
Fiat Economics 102: What is labor/time?	22
Fiat Economics 103: What are Taxes?	24
Fiat Economics 104: What is Intergenerational Debt?	26
Fiat Economics 105: Potato Economics	28
Modern Monetary Theory Through Potato Economics	28
Chapter 3 – A Nation of Individuals	31
The State: A Community of Communities	34
America: A Nation of Communities	35
Chapter 4 – Education: Top Quality for Students, Parents, and Teachers	38
Who Should Public Education Serve?	39
A More Equitable Plan	40
4 – Step Transition	41

Chapter 5 – Healthcare	47
Healthcare Insurance	47
Healthcare or Insurance?	48
Road Blocks to Affordable Healthcare	49
Crony Licensure	52
An Immediate Solution	53
Chapter 6 – Rehabilitating A Prison System	58
Research	58
The Cure	60
Chapter 7 – Energy Costs, Production, and Innovation	61
Maine's Carbon Footprint	61
Where We Get Our Power	62
Chapter 8 – Fixed Income: Retired, Disabled, and Robbed	64
Costs	64
What Can We Do	68
Further Considerations	69
Chapter 9 – Maine-Based Retirement	71
Considerable Data	71
Chapter 10 – The Forest for The Trees	75
Government Control Destroys Workers' Futures	75
Redistribution	76
Bonds	76
Bureaucracy	77
Chapter Last - Your Choice, Your Voice, Our Future	80

Preface

The Wrong Enemies

Civil War – We Are 2 Maines

There are two Maines, the clearest proof of two Maines is the 2016 presidential electorate map. Why we split so clearly is not because some people are ignorant, evil, racist, vile, or deplorable snowflakes, but rather because we are a nation of diverse values. We have been led to think of urban and rural communities as at war (and thus, we are at war). Our puppet masters have taught us that our values cannot be realized if we allow their values to exist... This narrative has enslaved us; if we are to be at war, we should be fighting the system of oppression not our friends and family.

Left and Right – A False Choice

Psychology is the study of behavioral and conditioning factors from our experiences which guide us to think how we think. As a Counseling Psychologist, I devote my studies to understanding how people think and why. In politics, people are often distracted and propagated into one corral or another based on 'truths' which are better defined as a spectrum. The irony is that left and right ideologies are not political, they are economic, and they need not be debated as an all or nothing but rather, they should be understood, adapted, and implemented as seen fit by the populations they affect.

Too often we are told that if your priorities are property rights, self-protection, and self-sovereignty, you are the enemy of those whose priorities are healthcare and education. This false dichotomy gets us into heated debates and perpetuates the notion that an enemy team lurks in wait to destroy your values.

The ideological perspective of politics has little to do with innate values, morality, or compassion/empathy and all to do with conditioning and self-service. Believing in the rights of others is selfless service; believing your worldview is better implemented on others than their personal desires and choices is oppression. Economic and self-serving concerns are justified as a species and an individual; oppression is unjustifiable.

Own or Rent?

Having lived in rented apartments and in an owned home, one can easily see the difference (though few notice it) in priorities and the reasons for the left/right paradigm.

Renters live in a constant and perpetual state of chaos. As someone else owns their residence, there is always a chance of being homeless at the whims of someone else. A home owner who rents to renters has certain guidelines they must legally follow before casting someone out into the street, but the general understanding is, when you are told to leave, you could be homeless. The nature of this chaos leaves a renter with their concerns in life having nothing to do with investment in the property they reside in. After all, knowing (perceiving) your home is temporary leaves the renter with little incentive to maintain the property or invest in the property. This lack of property investment has a broad range; many renters will let the walls and paint of their apartment degenerate, will not clean their apartments, or may leave the apartment in such disarray and filth that rot and damage comes to the apartment. Ultimately, the renter's values shift away from the land, the property, and away from concerns of protecting the property from damage, theft, or oppression.

What remains after dissociating yourself from property rights and the necessary tools for protecting that property is concerns with self. Renters value their body and minds over property and property protection. Given this conditioned focus, we can easily see how urban areas are more likely to value healthcare and education than other values. As a renter, someone who can only count on themselves being the consistent factor in their lives, the conditioning of self-service through mind and body protections is easy to realize.

Similarly, those in rural areas tend toward the values of property protections and the means of defending that property. As a property owner, you pour work and money into the future of your property. Looking to the future for a home owner is estimating that future value of your property or planning on growth from the land itself. Farmers look to the ground as an investment, knowing that their efforts in landscaping, adding nutrients, and planting crops will add to the prosperity of the land. A land owner sees their land as the constant in their future.

Land owners are thus prone to defend property rights, self-protection rights, and encourage a deregulation (lessened oppression) of their property. While the land owner is concerned with their health and education, the two are secondary to the promise of their property as the property and their investments in the property will (theoretically) out live them.

Left and right dichotomies are a farce. The idea that heeding one person's values will oppress yours is a game played to enforce our continued warfare. The leadership driving the sales of political ammunition stay in power while the slave class fights itself. We can do better but it takes some perspective and will.

Rural Mainers can realize their property, self-protection, and sovereignty rights while concurrently, urban Mainers can realize their healthcare and educational rights. Understanding where these rights are derived from makes all the difference. At the community level, there is zero reason that urban, coastal Mainers cannot install community spending and community provision

Your Choice, Your Voice, Our Future - Richard Lee Light

of expanded redistributions for purposes of education and healthcare while rural Mainers implement and maintain reduced property oppression and continued property defense. The two have nothing to do with one another unless your plan includes one community dictating what the other should do.

Other than oppression, aggression, and extortion there is no way that a rural community would be able to force urban communities (or vice versa) into living under their economic ideology. This battle, this civil war, is doing nothing but ensuring the centralized power of the warmongering class remains in power while we remain slaves.

Work toward a community who recognizes and strives for your personal values while resisting the work of authoritarians and fascists who would force your compliance with their world view. We are free if we fight for it.

Prologue

Stopping

There are two ways to stop a moving vehicle: either you put a wall in front of the vehicle and it stops immediately (saving neither the car nor the passengers), or, you apply brakes until the car has slowed enough to stop (which is clearly less immediate yet drastically more reasonable). – Richard Light 2016

Ending the usury and abuse of a heavily bureaucratic, crony, and enslaving system is easily declared best removed through an immediate and absolute method ("End the fed", "abolish the IRS", and "smash the State" are a few such examples of rhetoric) but does nothing for the reality of those who would be left to fend for themselves in the process. Those reliant on social programming are (like a domesticated pet) incapable of functioning without the support of those programs (the hand that feeds them).

Often the reliance debate becomes one of humility versus humanity. Those with the capabilities of survival without government see the debate as one of humility, often reciting words of distain for 'lazy, entitled leaches' as they view the reliance on government for their survival as a choice born of lack of will rather than lack of ability

On the other side is the conditioned recipient of services and governmental support. If anyone contests that we are animals and programmed through our experiences, please review some other works (Behaviorism: John Broadus Watson published "psychology as the behaviorist views it"; Classical conditioning: John Watson; Operant conditioning: B.F. Skinner). Through the positive reinforcements of government care (eating food, receiving healthcare, the feeling of a check in the mail, parental relief from sending a child to school or to daycare), those who receive governmental assistance are actively conditioned to appreciate the service. But, this conditioning goes further as the longer the services are provided, the more reliant the recipient becomes. Seeing this in a humane way, the longer a citizen is subject to this 'care', the more incapable they become without it.

- After 2 years, an unemployed worker becomes normalized, working becomes harder than be funded to stay home (reemployment rates drop over time)
- After 2 decades, a child who knows nothing more than that a check on the 10th will pay for food and housing sees this as the way to be fed and stay housed (generational reliance)
- After 2 generations, a society which sends children away for 36 hours a week begins to care less about the content of their child's day and instead sees an interruption of the ease in this service (dropping a child off in the AM and retrieving them in the PM) as an inconvenience.

The blame of dependence can be viewed as apathy, greed, and selfishness or dependence can be viewed as a necessary and predictable response to years, decades, or generations of conditioning. Perception is reality; your perception defines your reality.

In order to end the reliance on government, it is unreasonable and irresponsible to attempt putting a wall in front of the figurative car. Those who are reliant are simply incapable of functioning in the current economic environment, as is current society incapable of adapting to them. In order to reinstate the dependent population as sovereign individuals (releasing them from the bonds of slavery), the process will take years, decades, and generations to be effective and autonomous.

Anarchist frenemies

The Agorist understands that creating a society in which all relations between people are voluntary (non-mandated and thus non-governed; freedom opposed to slavery), means counter-economics and peaceful revolution. The Agorist applies the brakes.

Reducing government power and returning power and authority to individuals does not include smashing the State. Contrary to the accepted ideology of Anarchists, smashing the system is not best for everyone. In reality, many people are not only content with servitude to the crown, but flourish through collectivism. Moving toward a free society does not include forcing individualism on everyone, moving toward a free society is nothing than allowing people to choose their level of servitude.

Separate, unequal, and free.

For a voluntary society to flourish, America would need to return toward the system of government we were given originally. Those who deny the path to freedom will claim that racism, patriarchies, and capitalism go hand in hand with America's founding image. The truth is however that the constructs of gender, race, and money are propagated obstructions to freedom. These concepts are written into the conditioning of slaves, contrary to the ideals of the founding image of America's government.

The United States government had simply the role of ensuring that individuals could trade with one another, live near one another, and live their values without oppression from their neighbor while independent of permissions from a master. After 2 centuries of conditioning, manipulation, and crony behavior, the system which clearly offered self-sovereignty to the individual has instead become a system of control lacking representation of the people; this system

Your Choice, Your Voice, Our Future - Richard Lee Light

now stands as a communistic system of oppression, the masses being subject to the extortion, wills, and whims of the ruling class elite. The United States government lacks to objective of protecting the people from oppression as it is now the agent of oppression.

A return to the founding ideal of the United States would be a society which values '3%', 'oath-keeping' 'homesteaders' as much as it values 'socialistic' 'collectivist' 'communes'. A principled United States government would stand only to protect one from the other, not be a force to punish and condemn those who's ideologies differ from their neighbors'. If America were free, Americans would live free: alone and self-reliant to densely collectivized but all sharing the freedom to make our own choices.

Moving the Needle

Moving the needle from slavery toward freedom requires only the will to begin the process. Fear of change is the major most obstacle in change. Fear is irrational and fear of change is most irrational. Inability to adapt to change is the primary result of societal conditioning. A conditioned slave appreciates the scraps of their masters and thanks their master for their benevolence between beatings. Conceiving freedom would stand against the comforts the slave has 'earned'. We are similarly stuck in servitude, and yet, the path to freedom begins with taking those first steps toward change.

There are several steps toward a free and voluntary Community, State, Nation, and world. Steps toward freedom at each level vary by their control, their leadership, their current and intended purpose, and the will and ability of those who would battle authoritarians. While I encourage and support others who would help move us toward freedom, it is only through the scope an American State which I offer a course of correction.

A complaint without a solution is nothing more than 'bitching', the following passages are proposed solutions. These solutions are more generally applicable than their presentation and will serve well to adapt as the battlefield and society adapts. While regarding proposals (these and all) for our government, read the proposal, make an objective review (seeing the forest for the trees rather than the immediate and self-gratuitous benefits), and weigh whether the proposal benefits one group at the cost of another, and whether autonomy (functioning alone by the actions of those who benefit) is attainable.

Your Choice, Your Voice, Our Future - Richard Lee Light

Chapter 1

A Game of Thrones

It has pained me to make it to a place in my life where I find it necessary to run for an office in order to impact the future. Through healthcare as a counselor, education as a teacher, through the Army as a soldier, as a corrections officer, and as a father I have wanted nothing more than for others to be free, educated, and prosperous. What I learned through each of these paths is that non-political people cannot help one another on a grand scale, we cannot use our knowledge, experience, and innovations to impact the systems which control us. In other words, a civilian is a cog within a very large machine; the machine of our nation is a collection of institutions controlled by bureaucrats and politicians. To effectively implement any positive changes to the machine means being a bureaucrat or a politician (or buying one). I do not seek an office for money or fame, I seek an office for the power. The power I seek is sought to offer innovations, deliver freedom back to the people, and use the podium of the office as a stage to present individual ideas. We as people have been silenced; I will not let this continue without a fight.

In reviewing the roles of government officials, I have made an effort over the last few years to attend and participate in every level of State Government. From town meetings to selectmen's meetings I was able to achieve reduced taxes and increased personal liberties while helping institute local initiatives in green energy, sovereign food, and social investments. As an avid defender in progress and fiscal responsibility, it was through my community that I found my voice. For anyone who wants to have an actual impact on taxes and how they are spent, it is only through local politics which our voices have the ability to directly affect social-spending. The further up the centralization ladder we move, the less voice we have. Please reference "Slave to Citizen" (2016) for more on my local initiatives.

At the State level I realized quickly that my voice had no weight. Reaching out to a district representative seems easy enough, so I did, several in fact. After some chats via emails and phones, I thought, "yes, there is someone who listened to me and told me they would bring up what they just agreed was worth a discussion." And yet, reality got in the way. Our representatives carry flags for their teams, regardless of the topic, regardless your experienced perspective on a topic, at the end of the day a district representative works only for the team they are on and only votes for what they are told to vote for. Standing against their team means they are taken off committees, they lose their precious team funding, and they are actively undermined by their teammates. Thus, we as people hold no power in the State House. Once our voice is being 'represented' rather than being directly heard, we cease to have a voice.

Like the State Representatives, State Senators are sometimes accessible via Email and Phone. Also, similar to representative seats, Senators are not beholden to the communities. As these offices require a thousand signatures to gain ballot access for, it is a very elite group who can get on the ballot. Since most contests are thus limited to the candidates presented from the two (corporately funded) teams, State Senators have no need to offer the innovations or ideas of the general public. Instead, State Senators retain their positions by doing what their team tells them to do. Since nearly 70% of their constituents are unenrolled or part of the opposing team, the wills of the majority are never part of their legislation.

The final nail in our coffin is federal level representation. The offices of a State's Senator or Congress-Person are so far removed from our voice that they needn't even respond to us when we call or e-mail. In fact, as a challenge, contact them about a policy you disagree with. Generally, you receive and automated email response to an email and a robocall (if any) to your phone call.

Your Choice, Your Voice, Our Future - Richard Lee Light

Since these offices cost millions of dollars to win (Maine's 2016 2nd district Senate seat cost $12,000,000), unless you are a major donor don't expect to even have an audience, let alone an impact on legislation. Further, ask yourself how the average Federal Elect somehow makes an average of 1.6 million dollars per year in office (the job averages $175,000 pay).

As I reviewed all this and participated to some frustrating ends, I reviewed my experience and my goals in helping the system. I looked at what the jobs are for each level of representative and what impact I might be able to make if I were elected to an office. As a taxpayer, I can participate and impact local policy just by showing up and speaking; in other words, there is no need to run for local office to affect positive change. In reviewing and trying to participate in State level offices, I was disheartened to realize that even with a district or county level position, the impact was small to inexistent in that one innovation will not make legislation. Without being within one of the two major teams, a legislator cannot actually even submit bills. Submitted bills that do not have support from the major teams' leaders are tabled (disregarded) or opposed. Committee seats are reserved for teammates and leadership positions within committees are held ransom for towing the team line. While many of our State reps are trying to make one good bill stick, they are forced to comply with dozens of crony bills and rarely (most often never) being able to submit bills which may actually help citizens.

Looking at my savings and the cost of getting on the ballot, I narrowed my attempted election run to one office. With experience and education in corrections, education, healthcare, and business, there is only one elected position which I feel I can offer power back to the communities, positively affect the institutions in which I am knowledgeable, and afford to run for. The stage is such that I will likely only have one shot at speaking publicly on behalf of these ideals. The election of a Governor is the contest which will offer me a stage to speak to you and our neighbors. It will cost me my savings (I am not beholden to any special interest and thus must fund this myself and through citizen donations), it may cost me future jobs as politics has a volatile side (negative campaigns and smear tactics), and it may cost me relationships. But, it will offer me a stage to voice my concerns and if we are successful in this, this election will offer us some of our freedom back, will provide a stage for more voices to be heard, and will move our system from an antiquated pyramid scheme to an innovative engine for economic and social prosperity.

A Governor's Job

What makes me think that a Governor's position is the best place to make an economic and liberating impact for citizens? Well, let's start by reviewing what their job entails, what they 'control', and how the Governor's governance can reach citizens while remaining accessible to the citizenry. Please consider the following citation from the National Governor's Association (2015):

Overview

As state managers, governors are responsible for implementing state laws and overseeing the operation of the state executive branch. As state leaders, governors advance and pursue new and revised policies and programs using a variety of tools, among them executive orders, executive budgets, and legislative proposals and vetoes.

Governors carry out their management and leadership responsibilities and objectives with the support and assistance of department and agency heads, many of whom they are empowered to appoint. A majority of governors have the authority to appoint state court judges as well, in most cases from a list of names submitted by a nominations committee.

Your Choice, Your Voice, Our Future - Richard Lee Light

Approval of State Budgets and Appropriations

Governors develop and submit annual or biennial budgets for review and approval by the legislature. In many states, commonwealths, and territories, governors also have "reduction"—most often referred to as "line-item"—veto power that can be used for the removal of appropriations to which they object. These tools allow governors and their budget staff to play a strong role in establishing priorities for the use of state resources.

Enactment of Legislation

Governors often use State of the State messages to outline their legislative platforms, and many governors prepare specific legislative proposals to be introduced on their behalf. In addition, state departments and agencies may pursue legislative initiatives with gubernatorial approval. Executive branch officials often are called to testify on legislative proposals, and governors and other executive branch leaders will seek to mobilize public opinion and interest groups in favor of or opposition to specific legislative proposals. Governors may use their role as party leaders to encourage support for legislative initiatives, and along with department heads and staff may seek to influence the progress of legislation through regular meetings with legislators and legislative officials.

Gubernatorial Appointments

Most governors have broad authority to nominate officials to serve in state executive branch positions—many of whom will be included in the governor's advisory committee, known as the "cabinet." Governors may be empowered as well to make appointments to state judgeships.

Frequently, these appointments are subject to confirmation by one or both houses of the state legislature. While often pro forma in nature, the confirmation process with respect to executive branch appointments can be used by legislatures to expand their influence on governors and their policies. Accordingly, many governors consult with key legislators before making formal nominations.

Boards and Commissions

The roles played by boards and commissions vary considerably by state and by program. In some states appointed boards have the primary responsibility for individual programs and agencies and are responsible for the selection of department and agency heads. This is particularly true in the field of education, but boards still retain responsibility for a broad range of other programs in fields such as labor, transportation and health and human services.

In many states the members of these boards are named or nominated by the governor. And in many of these cases, board members are subject to confirmation by one or both houses of the legislature.

Other boards play more limited regulatory or advisory roles. In most states boards oversee the licensing and regulation of numerous professions and business areas. In other states, they advise the governor on areas of importance such as the environment and economic development.

My Goals as Governor

Now, understanding that a Governor's role has much to do with our institutions (budgets, policies, staff, and implementation), it should be very clear why I am seeking this office. With a focus on individualism, education, healthcare, and corrections, my proposed innovations intend to return communities to power while opening our institutions to working for children, the sick, and those in need rather than for the benefit of a few well-connected elites.

Each specific initiative is more clearly and fully defined in the following chapters.

Reference

National Governors Association (2015) Governors' Powers and Authority. More information at:

https://www.nga.org/cms/home/management-resources/governors-powers-and-authority.html

Chapter 2
Fiat Economics – A Beginner's Guide

This chapter is a course in some monetary basics. It is too often a reminder when people speak that they do not have the core understanding of what money is, what taxes are, what economics is, and what generational debt (the national debt) is. Let this chapter serve as a basic overview or a reminder.

Fiat economics 101: What is money?

What is money?

1) a current medium of exchange

Meaning simply, money is the paper, coin, or digital exchange that represents our labor and or property; money is an easily made and easily regulated form of physical representation for the intangible idea that labor, time, and property belong to one person and should be exchangeable, tradable, or donatable to another person or entity.

Money is known as "fiat" meaning it is not worth the material it is printed on and is hence only as valuable as the concept of its value (unlike gold or silver). The worth of money is governed by the printing entity (usually a government) and fluctuates by the amount of fiat currency within a system of exchange. If a system has too much fiat currency, the value of it goes down and it costs more to buy things or labor.

The dollar as we know it is printed by the U.S. treasury and is loaned out or taken in by the federal reserve (a private bank). The loaning of new money from the federal reserve to banks adds money to the banks for loans to people (lowering the value of the dollar, decreasing what money is worth, and making money you have or make worth less). Conversely, when the federal reserve recollects money from banks, the value of your money goes up (your bank account is worth more, your hourly wage is worth more, and the money you spend can buy more).

Because we use a fiat monetary system, the power of the dollar is highly controlled, easily manipulated, and dangerously fragile. Should the federal reserve increase the flood of fiat currency into the system (say for instance it gave out a million dollars to everybody) the value of the dollar would become worthless.

Economic theories begin here: two main factions of thinking exist based on the above information being carried into the real-life system of loans, spending, and growth.

1. Keynesian economics: The idea that every dollar that is loaned out from the federal reserve ripples into more than one dollar within the economy.
2. Austrian economics: The idea that every dollar that is loaned out from the federal reserve profits ideas that should have failed when they ran out of money.

The core difference is that Austrian economists believe that fiat money makes people's savings accounts diminish over time, companies and banks which should have gone broke from failed ideas would go broke if not propped-up by fiat money, and intergenerational debt is created through the system of fiat currency.

Keynesian economists believe that constant inflation (which the federal reserve maintains at at-least 2%) ensures that new workers can have access to new wealth, fiat currency cycles through the economy in an overlapping fashion (which means the dollar is worth several dollars as it is used several times), and that the control over inflation and wealth through the federal reserve ensures an economic collapse cannot occur.

The debate on economics will continue and both sides will continue to be right and wrong. As with most ideologies, somewhere between the two is usually where we end up and coincidentally, it is where we flourish. This passage is not all inclusive, nor is it in your best interests to stop learning after a basic introduction; read more, learn more.

Fiat Economics 102: What is labor/time?

If we recall from Fiat Economics 101, fiat money is the physical manifestation of a medium used for trading labor and/or property for property and/or labor. We quite literally use our time dedicated to work toward earning banknotes which we trade for stuff.

The concept which is often lost in this discussion is that work = time:

Work is an application of the worker's time (something we can never get back) traded for money. Our time is invaluable as every second we lose in life can never be recovered, sending us closer to death and never offering us more life than we had one second ago.

Compensation for our time is an endless debate:

- Some theorists believe people should be compensated for time at equal rates regardless of the toughness or productivity of our work. See Communism.
- Some theorists believe people should be compensated for time based on how valuable our work is. See Capitalism.
- Some theorists believe people should be compensated for time whether productive, self-serving, or idle. See Socialism.

Your Choice, Your Voice, Our Future - Richard Lee Light

- Some theorists believe people should not be compensated and that all labors should be spent toward the betterment of society as whole. See Marxism.

The main theories have little in common. Marxists believe that your labor (your time) belongs to everyone. Socialists believe that not everyone should work but that everyone deserves some reward from the labors (time) of those that do work. Communists believe that all people should work hard but hard work should only benefit society. Capitalists believe that if you work and donate your time, you should receive compensation for it and be entitled to keep what you worked for.

The themes are consistent in all forms of economic ideology: people work and work creates wealth. The differences are firmly set in who profits from the time people use of their lives to work. What is consistent is that those who work the most (using hours of their lives they will never have back) tend to want compensation for their time while those who do not work (keeping their time for themselves) tend to expect compensation from others' labors (time).

As with all systems of ideology, we live in a hybrid system; labor is compensated to the worker and the non-worker. Time given and lost by the worker is divided between themselves and society. The debate we tend to have is: how much of someone's labor (time) is another person entitled to?

Fiat Economics 103: What are taxes?

Tax: a financial charge or other levy imposed upon a taxpayer (an individual or legal entity) by a state (Government) or the functional equivalent of a state (Government) to fund various public expenditures. A failure to pay, or evasion of or resistance to taxation, is usually punishable by law.

There are several types of taxes:

- Income tax: a portion of workers' labor (time). See Fiat Economics 102
- Property tax: a portion of home owner's property. See Fiat Economics 101
- Sales tax: a portion of property which has changed hands from one human to another.
- Payroll taxes: 'income tax', renamed and taken so the laborer does not see the bill.
- Consumption tax: 'sales tax', renamed and taken from the purchaser rather than the seller.
- Capitation: a fixed, perpetual cost for living or providing/using a service.

Taxes other than Capitation (a rare form of taxation promoted and used in the healthcare industry) are radically different in who pays them, how they are generated, and what they are used for. This lesson is not about government spending and thus only focusses on the generation of taxes.

Income tax: Having all your labor (time) taken from you for the benefit of someone other than you is called slavery. Having some of your labor taken from you to benefit someone other than you is called income tax. The concept of income tax is often a battle between workers and non-workers as workers (people who give up their time to labor) are taxed, while people who do

Your Choice, Your Voice, Our Future - Richard Lee Light

not work (people who do not give up their time to labor) are not forced to donate labor (time) to others.

The battle over income tax has clear reasoning as an unfair and biased tax. In a Capitalist or Socialist system (See Fiat Economics 102) a limited portion of society is forced to labor (donate their time) while the other portion is not; this imbalance creates tension as one person is forced to work for others while another person works for no one; both people receive compensation yet only one loses their life's limited time while the other loses nothing.

Property tax: Property is a finite commodity (there is only a certain amount). People reside on property whether they own the property or not. Renters and home owners both pay property tax (homeowners pay this directly while renters pay this through their landlord).

Several forms of property tax exist. Zoning is a community level regulation dictating what types of housing or businesses may be built, occupied, or run on select properties within a community. Some properties pay more in taxes (such as waterfronts and some businesses), while other properties pay less or none at all (Churches, swampland, woodlots, and incentivized businesses). Regardless of which properties are taxed and not taxed, the cost of the community as a whole is paid for by the generation of property taxes. The measures which determine the costs of property tax are equal for equally valued and zoned properties.

Sales tax: Transferring property from one person to another is taxed at varied levels depending on the type of property, the location of the transfer, the amount of property transferred, and sometimes other factors. Sales tax affects only those who transfer property through a fiat currency exchange which is monitored by the governing entity; private transfers of property which are not monitored or reported to any authority or fiat-regulating-entity are not taxed.

Sales taxes create black markets where property transfers are hidden so as to avoid taxation. Sales taxes are higher for persons who purchase property more than another person, and sales taxes are a method of systemic control of property transfers which the governing entity may use to control who is allowed to own what and where that property may be allowed (for instance, liquor sales are controlled by time of day they are allowed, entitlement to purchase, and higher costs on purchasers in an attempt to reduce or limit their consumption).

Payroll taxes and consumption taxes: These taxes are duplicates of income taxes and sales taxes except that they are taken from employers and purchasers rather than employees and sellers. These taxes are often a form of double taxation which are intended to avoid scrutiny since they are gathered form a smaller number of persons and less visible than income or sales taxes.

Tax fairness is always questionable in that they are not equal; some people work more, some people own more, and some people purchase more. What percentage of income taxation is slavery, what level of property taxation becomes government preventing people from owning land, and what level of sales tax creates black markets and destroys property transfers (markets)?

Fiat Economics 104: What is Intergenerational Debt?

We are born into slavery through a debt which is stolen back from us as forced, extorted labor throughout our entire lives. We are slaves to a debt we neither made, nor spent, nor contracted. We are slaves to the debts of our parents, we are slaves to the debts of a Corporation (the United States Government), and we are slaves to the debts burdening the United States' as a result of corporate bailouts, bonds (government loans), and Corporate-Government deficits. We are slaves to the private, World-Bank, the privately owned "political" system, and Keynesian Modern-Monetary-Theory.

> *Debt bondage (also known as debt slavery or bonded labor) is a person's pledge of their labor or services as security for the repayment for a debt or other obligation. The services required to repay the debt may be undefined, and the services' duration may be undefined. Debt bondage can be passed on from generation to generation.*

Millennials of the United States are born into 48,000 dollars of debt in 2016. An infant who breathes their first breathe is born with a debt which they never agreed to, never benefit from, and can never repay. When Millennials become working age, their share of the intergenerational debt is more than 87,000 dollars. By the time Millennials are able to take on their first full time employment, the debt they must begin to pay off, a debt which doubles every 9 years, is deducted from their labors at approximately 35%. In other words, a Millennial must work 14 hours a week (for no pay) to sustain the current interest on their intergenerational debt. The debt itself does not go down; the interest on the debt continues to accumulate; the burden of the debt continues to devalue the money Millennials earn, reducing the power of their dollar to buy anything; the government continues to borrow on the behalf of children yet born; and the debt of the generation to follow is more than that of the generation who did the borrowing.

Fiat Economics 105: Potato Economics

The theory of Keynesian economics and Modern Monetary theory is that a government borrowing money on the behalf of the future generation would be able to invest the borrowed money in order for it to grow as an investment, netting not only a gain for the generation that spends the money but also increasing the value of the borrowed money to benefit the generation which will inherit the debt (and supposed interest).

Modern Monetary Theory through Potato Economics:

What is supposed to happen:

1) I borrow 10 potatoes from my son.

2) I plant the borrowed 10 potatoes (invest them) and grow 100 potatoes over the course of 18 years.

3) My son is handed the 10 potatoes when he turns 18; he is also handed the interest of 90 potatoes which I owe him as interest on his investment.

4) My son is nine times better off than he would be when he turned 18 if I had never invested his potatoes on his behalf.

What actually happens:

1) I borrow 10 potatoes from my son.

2) I eat or otherwise consume and use the potatoes.

3) I gain more at the cost of my son and with that I can retire, live beyond my means, and suffer no burden, but instead show a gain in my life for the act of borrowing from my son.

Your Choice, Your Voice, Our Future - Richard Lee Light

4) My borrowing incurs interest, which becomes a debt of 100 potatoes when my son turns 18.

5) My son turns 18, inherits the debt of 100 potatoes, and forever more must work to pay down the debt and interest which he has been saddled with on my behalf.

The theory of borrowing from your children has roots in a philosophically stable ideology, but the reality of implementation has proven that stealing from your children benefits you now and enslaves them later.

The national debt of the United States is not mine, it is not my generation's debt, and its continued growth through devaluation and interest is no more than generational slavery imposed on us through a private corporation (The United States Government) handing our futures to Bankers (through pay-outs), Corporations (through subsidies), and to America's Communistic Institutions (through bonds and bureaucrat entitlements).

The general population thinks they benefit from these "investments". The illusion is that social security, Medicaid, and other programs are investments in the future which will benefit all persons to be born and live in the United States. The reality is that programs that help the generation of today were invested in by the generation of today and should have been solvent in the taxes paid by the generation of today. The National debt is in fact only a money laundering scheme by which the future generation is stolen from for the current generation's bankers, politicians, bureaucrats, and corporate elites to benefit. These bankers, politicians, bureaucrats, and corporate elites invest the money they steal on their own behalf. The result is that the bankers, politicians, bureaucrats, and corporate elites gain interest while the generations who were stolen from gain more debt.

We will never pay this debt. We cannot work enough hours for free to pay down this debt. As it is, Millennials work 14 hours per week as slaves to the bankers, politicians, bureaucrats, and corporate elites which stole our money, and with it, our futures.

Moreover, the math is even worse when you consider that 40% of Millennials are unemployed and 40% of Millennials are under-employed (part-time, low-wage). These numbers mean our generational debt is increasing far faster than we are gaining means to pay for it. The result is that the debt will grow beyond our ability to even manage the interest (projected for 2018-2020). We are broke as a nation; we continue to borrow on generations who are not yet born, our national budget exceeds our national income every year which further buries us in more and more debt.

Being born to debt and having your labor stolen from you for the rest of your life to pay for a debt you never incurred is slavery. There is no other definition but slavery which fits the model our government has imposed on its people. Our masters are bankers, politicians, bureaucrats, and corporate elites who have benefited from and continue to benefit from our slave-debt.

This cannot continue, this will not continue. Either we stand against this debt or we endure our slavery until the debt collectors collect. Be it an international force of countries which invade and occupy our nation as our new masters, or be it that the private bankers who manipulated this debt into our slavery capitalize directly on their control by stealing the remainder of our labors (this is actually happening now as we have to work more and more to pay the minimum slave-debt), if we do not rise against this debt and slavery, we will no longer able to be able to fight for our freedom.

Your Choice, Your Voice, Our Future - Richard Lee Light

Chapter 3
A Nation of Individuals

This passage is not a plan nor some kind of innovation...this passage is simply words of our founders and other political philosophers coupled with a layman's foundational understanding of how America was designed. If this passage feels too aloof for you (too much like philosophy of ideology), enjoy discovering the purpose of the Constitution and our role as Sovereign States. Take a minute to consider that regardless of your non-violent ideology (Libertarian, Socialist, Voluntarist, Democrat, Republican, Green), you are supported in your goals to live as you see fit while others are as well protected to live out their ideology. Our system was built to withstand the oppression of others but we are losing that protection. The more centralized our system becomes, the less individualism we are allowed. Monarchs and fascists are consuming America, we can stand against this but it takes a basic Constitutional understanding.

"It takes time to persuade men to do even what is for their own good."

Thomas Jefferson

How do the ideas of communal property and private property, Anarchism and Communism, Capitalism, and Socialism (generally conflicting societal desires) all fit into a common political orientation?

After inquiring as to the commonalities in all these thoughts, it was only in non-aggression principles and decentralized government that all fell under the blanket of protecting the diversity of socio-political ideologies in America.

America is the perfect entity for encouraging and promoting a unified and coherent political protection of differing ideologies, the trick is adherence to the federal Constitution, as written regarding federal powers and oversight of the State's rights, and solidifying power of communities within the community of a State.

"Every government degenerates when trusted to the rulers of the people alone. The people themselves are its only safe depositories."

Thomas Jefferson

Individual rights refer to the liberties of an individual to pursue life and goals without interference from other individuals or the government.

"Individual rights are not subject to a public vote; a majority has no right to vote away the rights of a minority; the political function of rights is precisely to protect minorities from oppression by majorities (and the smallest minority on earth is the individual)."

Ayn Rand

Your Choice, Your Voice, Our Future - Richard Lee Light

A group of individuals will be drawn together based on commonalities in morals, ideals, and desires. We live this experience and see it present in research which has consistently shown that people tend to associate with people of like minds (Kassin S., Fein S. & Markus H., 2010).

What we find then is that we are naturally inclined to form communities as a part of human nature. Communities given the option of self-governing will be moralistically, idealistically, and desirously inclined to generate a community with the wants, laws, and reflection of life, liberty, and happiness of the individuals within the community.

In this way, communities may define their community, their industry, their housing, and community wealth. It is in the power of a community in which Anarchies, Democracies, Republics, Socialist-States, Communistic States, and ideals unmentioned can all exist and co-exist as neighbouring communities.

> *"A wise and frugal government, which shall restrain men from injuring one another, shall leave them otherwise free to regulate their own pursuits of industry and improvement, and shall not take from the mouth of labor the bread it has earned."*
>
> *Thomas Jefferson*

Because we are all so different and not one entity can effectively govern the life, liberty, and happiness of all the individuals of a system, it is in the interests of every individual to be governed by as small an entity as possible.

Each community is empowered to govern their community with the laws, benefits, and costs in which the community collects and delineates.

"Taste cannot be controlled by law."

Thomas Jefferson

This individualism and community empowerment can realize all the dreams of retirement and social welfare a community desires. With a group of likeminded individuals donating their labors to the realization of their entitlements, the community will regulate and manage their programs. It is in local control which the most financial reliability occurs; it is in local control that retirement funds, medical health costs, social welfare, emergency housing, environmental protections, and reliable responsibility will occur.

The State: A community of Communities

"Leave no authority existing not responsible to the people."

Thomas Jefferson

Intercommunity commerce, trade disputes, and aggression are reasons that a State is needed in a world of communities. Where it is one community's desire to be peaceful, make fair trade, and be cooperative with their neighbours, communities based on differing ideals may be

Your Choice, Your Voice, Our Future - Richard Lee Light

less inclined to work cooperatively with other communities. A State (a community of communities) offers a voluntary membership of communities where the individual communities can reallocate or donate money, services, or resources to the State for the purpose of judging and enforcing fair trade and non-aggression between communities (towns and cities).

As the people are responsible to their community for the means to run their community so too are the communities responsible for providing the means of the State to perform its services to communities. Just as communities have law enforcement, so too can the State. Just like communities have rules for trade so too will the State. The laws governing the State are derived of the communities, the means for assisting the State in its purposes are donated by the communities, and thus the regulation of the State is done by the communities.

Service is more responsive, less monetarily coercive, and morally responsible directly to the communities and by extension, the people. There is no better oversight of the system than by the people.

"The overwhelming majority of the American people know that we have got to stand together, that we're going to grow together..."

Bernie Sanders

America: A Nation of Communities

Why does it seem that our nation, the United States, lends so well to the idea of free and sovereign communities residing within larger communities called States? That one is easy and history, our founders wrote our law to be a nation contrived this way.

> "I have no fear that the result of our experiment will be that men may be trusted to govern themselves without a master."
>
> Thomas Jefferson

America's laws were initially written with such clarity regarding life, liberty, and happiness that dictatorial desires by those elected to govern had to drastically change the documents to reflect their biases and persona desires. Our initial documents and laws have been so removed from what they were intended to be that our system is facing an identity crisis. What most people now feel is a failed system is in fact a failed editing of our system. The provisions are there for our nation to be empowered by the communities, and in the same way our States are empowered by those communities, so too is the federal government.

We have lost our power to be separate from the State. We have been forced to pay for the operation of a war machine for so long; we do not see that it is our right to not pay it. Our freedom is not contingent on the federal government; it is in the community and the strength of our communities to unite. The federal government of the United States is only that, an entity empowered by 'united' States ('united' communities).

Removing the self-serving laws that detract from the individuals of this country, we will all find our community (be it anarchist, democratic, a republic, a society, or commune). What it takes is freeing ourselves from the machine that turned Corporations into people, reallocates the labors from every man woman and child (even those yet to be born) into pools of wealth for officials and corporations, and serves to destroy the planet around us with no remorse.

Your Choice, Your Voice, Our Future - Richard Lee Light

Our Nation was designed with the ability to offer every human a chance at a free life. We must find personal strength, bind together as communities, and seek to take what is ours from our masters. We need to take the power back!

Chapter 4
Education: Top Quality for Students, Parents, and Teachers

The issues with public education are many and the solution is actually very simple. What is difficult to achieve is undoing the crony oligarchy dictating the public's concept of what education is and what education must be. Propaganda, like in all aspects of today's societal manipulation, is a network expanding into our living rooms and living in the minds of our elderly and children. Teachers and administrators are held hostage by Stockholm, tax payers are seen as greedy enemies if they do not support 100% extortion and redistribution into the State's ill-spent bank account, and ultimately each generation loses ground in the battle for good teachers and quality education against the tidal waves of more and ever-growing bureaucracy and standardized mediocrity.

What Maine offers education is quality teachers and an experienced system of educating educators. While most Americans have complaints against the Department of Education (which the propagandists claim are battle cries against teachers and kids) not many Americans have a complaint about all teachers (sure, complaints about specific teachers do exist). In fact, most Americans (and especially most Mainers) have nothing but positive regard for the work, dedication, and abilities of educators.

Our issues in education are not teachers, the issues are in curricula, a one-size-fits-all model (i.e. no one should surpass the least capable student), teacher to student ratios, focus on standardized test results, and an inability to adapt education to the child's unique learning style. All of these issues are easily rectified.

Who should public education serve?

Providing the best system of education should have only one focus: How does the best result come to the children being educated?

Why am I, a parent, unable to spend the 16,000$ my child is worth to the Department of Education (Light, 2016) on quality teachers and a proven, effective curriculum? Who does this money benefit if not my child? Why does the system pit teachers against tax payers? Why do quality teachers not make enough money?

1) Teachers are underpaid by tens of thousands of dollars per year:

    a. Maine educators average 12 students per teacher (192,000$ per classroom)

    b. Maine teachers fight to make middle wage, averaging a $44,731 income

    c. Classrooms with 6 kids should be worth $72,000 (1/2 the kids, nearly twice the pay)

2) Learning results are better when the system has options:

    a. Students from private schools on average outperformed students from public schools in mathematics and reading achievement (U.S. DoE, 2011)

    b. Parent involvement programs that are instituted in traditional bureaucratic and inflexible school environments are less likely to yield positive results than those that are part of a more collaborative organizational structure (Comer and Haynes, 1991).

    c. Every child in America deserves a high-quality education, regardless of family income, ability, or background. If children are not learning and schools do not improve, parents should have options, including sending children to better public schools, charter schools, or private or parochial schools (House of Representatives, 2002)

3) The Maine teacher's union annually (The Center for Union Facts, 2016):

    a. Takes more than 11,000,000$ away from schools and students

    b. Spends more than 3.6 million dollars on its 72 employees

    c. Dumps over $4 million into politicians and lawyers to steal more money from students for the benefit of bureaucrats and plutocrats.

A More Equitable Plan

This proposed Educational plan offers teachers more money, children better results, parents better options, and Maine a system that is more in-line with being in the 21st century.

This plan does not propose taking money from anyone who directly teaches and positively affects children; this proposal proposes putting the money we already spend into an effective system that rewards teachers, has better learning results, prepares our children for a better future, and encourages parents from across the globe to send their children to Maine for an unmatched, quality education.

This plan immediately adds thousands of jobs to the market, increases the pay of quality instructors, offers parents more resources and more investment in their children's futures,

Your Choice, Your Voice, Our Future - Richard Lee Light

empowers students to learn skills for this century, and moves us toward a more expansive and inclusive educational system without adding one cent to tax payer's tax bills.

4-Step Transition

Implementing a quality, innovative, specialized educational program in Maine is as easy as 4 steps:

Step 1: The market place

- Currently, Maine parents only have choices for teachers and schools based on where they live and how much they can personally pay. The current monopoly system has limited options, poor results, no method for weeding out poor instructors, and zero options for a high-quality, personalized education for kids of parents with low income or urban residence.
    - A marketplace empowers teachers and parents.
    - When parents have personal investment in their child's education, their learning results are better; Parents being directly invested in the selection of quality instructors provides a foundation for parental involvement (Comer and Haynes, 1991).
    - Allowing Teachers the option of offering their skills and expertise directly to parents through a marketplace will allow parents to customize their child's education. A marketplace allows teachers to set their prices, choose their class size, and offer their specialized teaching methods directly to parents.
    - A marketplace gives parents the power. Parents can shop for high-quality instructors in topics that matter to their child's future. Children with needs outside

of the standard learning system can find instructors who specialize in their child's needs (hyperactive, special needs, gifted and talented).

- More teachers can earn more pay, provide better and more specialized service, have lower burnout rates, improve the quality of the educational system, and work in an environment where they are rewarded for hard and quality work within an education marketplace.

Step 2: Qualify instructors

1. Expand work and educational experience:

- Qualifying for a teacher's position in Maine has little to do with your degree or experience; instead, teachers are chosen based on who they know and where they went to school while those who have degrees and experience from outside this circle are denied positions.

  - Degrees in a science should help qualify a candidate for a Science teacher's position.

  - A degree in English should help qualify a candidate for an English teacher's position.

  - Being an Ed Tech or tutor for years and decades should count toward qualifying to be a teacher.

  - Expanding the specializations of educators offers more diverse instruction at higher quality.

  - More children are better educated when teachers are uniquely qualified in specialized instruction methods.

Your Choice, Your Voice, Our Future - Richard Lee Light

Step 3: Expand

- The system of education we have in Maine is antiquated and is only able to grow when we tax people; our system has no incentive or ability to innovate for the future.
  - This system will allow education to expand beyond the limited funding structure we use now; parents can supplement the costs for more classes or higher quality instruction while parents from across State borders would be able to invest money into buying instruction for their children.
  - Maine would experience unprecedented growth in education and provide tens of thousands of teaching positions while instructing millions of Americans with an innovative and specialized instruction worthy of the 21st century.
  - Expansion of our educational system lowers the costs and offers Maine tax payers increased tax revenues (more jobs and more residents) which reduces the tax burden on current residents while increasing the overall funding of education.

Step 4:   Assess build on what works while correcting what doesn't

- If your child is unable to learn in their classroom, has a low-quality or destructive teacher, or has needs that go beyond the 'average' student, your child suffers, stays back, does not gain a quality education, and loses out as an adult on jobs, college, and a future. In the system we have now, the parent, the child, and the tax-payers are blamed when schools fail.

- A system which measures quality, encourages what works, and removes what does not work is a system which offers the best results.

- Maine will lead the nation in educational quality, innovation, specializations, dynamics, and employment of quality teachers.

- Parents in Maine will have a say and added investment in their child's education, increasing learning results, improving the relationships between communities and teachers, and enriching the futures of Maine graduates.

- Maine will experience growth in our economy as teachers and parents from around the nation clamor to Maine looking for the best instruction and the best pay.

Operational costs (i.e. infrastructure) are to be noted in this plan as well. Infrastructure for education currently includes bus services, extracurricular programs, buildings, and teaching materials. This plan factors for operational costs in several ways:

- Currently, parents bear the burden of costs for extracurricular activities, averaging 739$ per child (White, 2016)

- Currently Maine Schools spend as much as 35,000$ for one student to be transported to school (Abbate, 2016)

  - Extracurricular activities will be acquired through the marketplace as coaches, teams, and other providers offer parents access to a broad array of activities, groups, and teams. While children currently have activity options limited by the school's budget and choices, the marketplace offers unlimited choices for activities, improving the health, inclusion, and college applications of Maine's students.

Your Choice, Your Voice, Our Future - Richard Lee Light

- Bus drivers are licensed through the State; this program ensures the same quality licensing is used for transporters of students. Transporters will utilize a separate section of the marketplace for securing transportation employment; this process will function identically to the other sections of the marketplace.

- Curriculums, licensing, space, and other learning materials are factors which potential teachers, teacher groups, or educational providers would be funding. As with all self-employment, start-up costs can vary; some teachers will have lower entry costs, some will have these materials provided by agencies, companies, unions, or collaboratives which they are employed or associated through.

Opposition to this system is irrational. Cronies, politicians, lobbyists, and bureaucrats who make money off educational funding while providing nothing to our kids stand to lose millions of dollars in this system. Teachers, administrators, community leaders, and Mainers of all walks stand behind this initiative as it gives our kids a better future, more options, an education for this century, provides better pay and incentives to teachers, and sets the stage for an economic and innovative boom in Maine.

"The future is here; our kids deserve to be a part of it." Richard Light 1998

References:

Light, Richard (2016) Cost of Education; retrieved at: http://light4me.org/maine-s-cost-of-education

The Center for Union Facts (2016) National Education Association, State Association - Maine Education; Spending: 2013; retrieved at https://www.unionfacts.com/lu/512668/NEA/0/#spending-tab

U.S. Department of Education, Institute of Education Sciences, National Center for Education Statistics, National Assessment of Educational Progress (NAEP) (2011) Mathematics and Reading Assessments.

James P. Comer and Norris M. Haynes (1991) Parent Involvement in Schools: An Ecological Approach; *The Elementary School Journal* Vol. 91, No. 3, Special Issue: Educational Partnerships: Home-School Community (Jan., 1991), pp. 271-277

House of Representatives, Subcommittee on the Constitution, Committee on the Judiciary (2002) Supreme Court's School Choice Decision and Congress' Authority to Enact Choice Program; 107th Congress 2nd session Serial number 101

Martha C. White (2016) Here's the Insane Amount the Average Parent Will Pay for After-School Activities; Times; Retrieved at http://time.com/money/4425114/parents-rising-costs-after-school-activities/

Lauren Abbate (2016) Unexpected special education costs prompt RSU 9 budget freeze; Kennebec Journal; retrieved at: http://www.centralmaine.com/2016/01/28/unexpected-special-education-costs-prompt-rsu-9-budget-freeze/

Your Choice, Your Voice, Our Future - Richard Lee Light

Chapter 5

Healthcare

Why we cannot afford a doctor or nurse is a question that we have been conditioned to avoid. Rather, we have been guided into a discussion and debate about whether we should have a pool of money available for healthcare if we become sick and need care. Many will say, "without the money, we won't be able to afford a doctor", and this is exactly why we are unable to find a solution.

We will dissect this topic and its many facets:

Healthcare Insurance

We see healthcare insurance as a safety-net where if we come down with an illness and we do not have the means to pay for care, we can use the group pool to cover the costs. Insurance works in this way because not everyone who pays into the pool will use the money. If 100 people pay 100$ into a pool (10,000$) and only 5 people use 2,000$ worth of the pool (10,000$) the pool worked as intended. Insurance companies use their banked capital to cover costs while they manage investments into the pool. If there is left over after the investments and payouts, they take home a profit. If an insurer does not make enough to cover the pool, not only do they go bankrupt, but those in the pool will pay and receive nothing. There is a great deal of risk in investing in insurance as an insurer; investing in insurance is beneficial in the event of catastrophe.

Insurance as a service is a good investment for the insured and can be profitable if competitive, measured, and managed with business savvy. Now, we all know someone who will throw a fit about profits being made (regardless of the industry) but that moves the conversation in another direction (one of slave ethics versus individualism, which is reserved for Chapter 3) and is not part of this conversation. Regardless of insurance, healthcare has a cost (the means of production: equipment has an investment and maintenance cost) as it takes labor by doctors, nurses, and other professionals to manually perform the labor; people who work should have compensation for their labor (otherwise it is slavery).

We can see the desire for healthcare insurance just as we see a value in car insurance. The difference is of course that purchasing car insurance is meant to reduce liability for the other driver should you be found at fault in a crash while health insurance is to cover yourself in the event of an illness, but, the value is clear regardless of purpose. But, as the purpose of healthcare insurance is self-protection and thus self-serving, so too should the choice of carrying health insurance as lack of it only affects the individual who chose to opt out.

Healthcare or Insurance?

Healthcare is NOT insurance. Healthcare is the labor by a Doctor, Counselor, Nurse, or other skilled practitioner when someone needs a service they are skilled in. Just as your plumber and mechanic is employed to fix your car or pipes, so too is a doctor employed for their knowledge and labor in fixing their patient. Compensation is expected for labor. When a person works for someone else to profit and makes nothing for their work, that is known as slavery.

What determines the compensation for healthcare providers and the costs of their work in general? That answer is not simple and continues to grow in its convolution. This question's answers will help us not only reduce the costs for care but open our nation to more and bountiful healthcare options. We could envision a $20 chemotherapy visit offered at 1000 places in your community, or we can continue to drive costs up and reduce providers; the shift from the current model (the latter) to the former requires understanding why things are as they are.

Road Blocks to Affordable HealthCare

Why does it cost 160$+ an hour for a doctor? Why is a Counselor 45$ an hour? Why is it 35-50$ an hour for a nurse? The costs to be a Doctor, Counselor, Nurse, or other professional do not begin when they find open an office. The costs to be a professional begin in the licensure department of our government. When a worker person decides to pursue healthcare as a profession, they are agreeing to meet the licensure requirements of their governmental bar. These bars are based on educational requirements, internships, and then testing and certification standards; as a result, we have a rationed pool of providers and thus a low supply and high demand (Costly).

The sales pitch for having a well-rounded and 'educated' professional is that to assure our doctor, nurse, or caregiver is competent and capable of delivering the service… or so we are led to believe. Let's dismantle this theory by its parts before estimating its sum:

Ethical practices: we are led to believe first and foremost that being a professional in healthcare means there is some kind of liability that can arise from improper care. If a doctor is unsafe or unethical, their client can be harmed or even killed. This is the core reason we have such high standards for becoming a doctor, nurse, or other caretaker. The sad reality is, there are injuries that occur for unethical and improper treatment and care regardless of the educational background of the professional since people are people and some people are simply unethical.

Regardless of the amount and type of education, unethical professionals still cause harm to people. Professionals are forced to carry insurance for their liability. The result is that unethical people get licenses and insurance companies pay for liability. The amount of ethics training offered and attended does not curb this process and does not make any unethical practitioner more ethical. Stating that education is a way to reduce liability from unethical behavior is not true.

A standardized/core education: we are often told the diversity of a core education is required in higher education in order to offer the student a better foundation for learning and innovative processing of information. The reality is that people have differing aptitudes for subjects; one person is phenomenal in math and has difficulties communicating ideas while another is a crafty empath but cannot manage to balance a long-term division equation. A "core" higher education serves two actual purposes and neither is for a more diversely innovative alumni: 1) core classes cost money and employ college professors in 100 level classes, ensuring their profitable profession continues to generate profits, and 2) forcing a core education as a requirement for higher education graduation reduces graduate volume, allowing those who do finish their degrees to have a smaller pool of competition in the workforce (allowing their 'value' to be higher; increasing the pay of graduates who find work).

In our discussion about the costs of a healthcare provider, this last bit of reality is the crux in why costs continue to rise for healthcare services. Not all people who have the aptitude to be a Doctor, Nurse, Social Worker, Counselor, or other professional are allowed to be if they cannot pass all levels of a core curriculum. While a doctor should have a strong science and mathematical capability, they may be denied graduation (and thus employment) for not having the ability to present a decent literature paper, pass a history class, or articulate the social advantages of interpersonal communication. Similarly, a potentially excellent, empathetic and socially impactful

Your Choice, Your Voice, Our Future - Richard Lee Light

person may not be able to graduate as a counselor if they cannot pass an algebra class. The core requirements of higher education are a money pit and an unnecessary roadblock to success.

We can see via just these 3 reasons why the costs of education are inflated to provide profit to schools and professors rather than provide a foundational education for the technical aspects of a job. Further costs of education are inflated through the crony practice of internships and residencies. We will delve more into residencies and internships further in this chapter, but as they stand, this practice serves no one but the educational institutions' profits. An internship is voluntary work (almost always unpaid) for an agency or healthcare provider. The student not only pays their school for this "class" but eats the cost of travel, food, housing, healthcare, and supplies while they work for free. Further, the supervisor within the agency of the intern is paid by their agency to supervise the intern; this is a cost to the agency for an employee that cannot generate income for the agency (since the intern lacks licensure and is non-billable for any services they do provide). While the experience is helpful in training new Social Workers, Nurses, and other professionals, this experience is costly.

Educational requirements are proven roadblocks for our poorest but capable citizens to become professionals. Because of the high costs of this exceptionally profitable industry, people are denied access to middle wage jobs if they cannot afford the education (many of which even loans will not cover because of the hundreds of thousands of dollars it costs) or the internships (which loans often will not cover since the costs are peripheral to schooling).

The largest obstacle for achieving a flourishing healthcare system is the profit-hungry higher educational system that stops it. Costs, cronyism, and rationing leave us with less Doctors, less Nurses, less Social Workers, and less healthcare providers. Since there is no fixed pie here (everyone gets sick) there is zero reason to ration healthcare provider education other than the money it generates.

Crony Licensure

Please consider: "The purpose of licensure is to protect the health, safety and welfare of the consumer public – not the profession. With few exceptions, only licensed individuals may practice in a regulated occupation or profession once a minimal degree of competency for public health, safety and welfare has been demonstrated." And: "Credentialing examination programs typically require prerequisite levels of education and/or experience prior to gaining entrance to the examination. These education and/or experience prerequisites form the basis of granting eligibility, or permission, to take the examination." (Association of Test Publishers, 2017)

This quote says a lot! First, we can see the clarity in which licensing examiners freely share the authoritarian nature of licensure. The sole purpose of licensure is to control the industries of "public health, safety, and welfare". More control of any industry directly correlates to reductions in available workers in that industry. Adding restrictions to the entry of a profession ensures less and less providers. I for one would prefer more doctors, nurses, counselors, and care providers... not less.

Next is the thought that a licensing test can ensure "competence" as the quote suggests. While there is some validity in stating that someone may not be able to pass a test without competency in the subject, the fact remains that if the test is offered to everyone, some people without the prequalifications for the test will be able to pass while others who have the prequalifications cannot pass the test. Testing can be useful but, to deny people who know the material and can pass the test, simply because they have not paid into the crony college system, is denial of good and qualified people based on their financial investment, not their quality. Further, denial of a candidate based solely on their lack of passing a test does nothing to offer quality

Your Choice, Your Voice, Our Future - Richard Lee Light

workers an opportunity to use their skills if they failed because of peripheral knowledge failures (such as lacking math skills in social working) or because of test anxiety. I would rather see an empathetic and effective counselor work and help addicts than deny them the opportunity because they cannot use the quadratic formula.

The final part of this statement to dissect is that licensure protects the health, safety, and welfare of a consumer. As noted earlier in this chapter: Regardless of the amount and type of education, unethical professionals still cause harm to people. Professionals are forced to carry insurance for their liability. The result is that unethical people get licenses and insurance companies pay for liability. The amount of ethics training offered and attended does not curb this process and does not make any unethical practitioner more ethical. The notion that a test can protect consumers is a fallacy and a dangerous one. We have a liability and law system, and the further we undermine it, the more likely it is to become useless. Would you rather have a licensed professional who, if they harm you, you cannot receive compensation and they can continue to practice on others? Or, would you prefer an unlicensed professional who, if they harm you, you can sue and they will be forced to stop harming others?

At every level, we see that licensure serves only to generate money for colleges, money for licensure departments, money for licensing test companies, and as a roadblock to diverse and affordable healthcare. Notions of safety and competence are diversions; we deserve affordable healthcare and better employment options, not a profit scheme.

An Immediate Solution

"Fixing" the costs of healthcare requires less regulation, not more (a notion standing in opposition to the propaganda wielding senses of too many people). Further, we need to separate from the concept of insurance BEING healthcare. Insurance helps pay for a high cost procedure, it is not a doctor. Once we begin to understand the foundations of the issue, we can better address some fixes.

Ending licensure would be a great start but honestly, the will for that is not here. Purists of liberty and the free-market must swallow the reality of public opinion and work (like the propogandists have done for decades) to change the will of the people. For now, we can make the system more inclusive so this is where we must begin our work.

Currently to be a professional, licensure requires educational requirements, interning/residency, and a test score. Experience, knowledge, and ability are not factors in the process of becoming Accountants; Auditors; Agents and Business Managers of Artists, Performers, and Athletes; Agricultural Inspectors; Appraisers and Assessors of Real Estate; Architects, Architectural and Engineering Managers; Athletes and Sports Competitors; Audiologists; Barbers; Bill and Account Collectors; Boilermakers; Chiropractors; Clinical, Counseling, and School Psychologists; Compliance Officers; Construction and Building Inspectors; Dental Hygienists; Dentists; Dietitians and Nutritionists; Earth Drillers, Except Oil and Gas; Education Administrators, Elementary and Secondary School; Education Administrators, Preschool and Childcare Center/Program; Educational, Guidance, School, and Vocational Counselors; Electrical Engineers; Electricians; Electronics Engineers; School Teachers; Emergency Medical Technicians and Paramedics; Environmental Engineers; Environmental Scientists and Specialists, Including Health; Explosives Workers, Ordnance Handling Experts, and Blasters; Family and General Practitioners; Farmworkers and Laborers, Crop, Nursery, and Greenhouse; First-Line Supervisors of Personal Service Workers; Food Batch makers; Food Service Managers; Funeral Service Managers; Furnace, Kiln, Oven, Drier, and Kettle Operators and Tenders; Gaming Cage Workers; Gaming Change Persons and Booth Cashiers; Gaming Dealers; Gaming Managers; Gaming Supervisors;

Your Choice, Your Voice, Our Future - Richard Lee Light

Geoscientists; Hydrologists and Geographers; Graders and Sorters, Agricultural Products; Hairdressers, Hairstylists, and Cosmetologists; Hazardous Materials Removal Workers; Health and Safety Engineers, Except Mining Safety Engineers and Inspectors; Heating, Air Conditioning, and Refrigeration Mechanics and Installers; Home Health Aides; Hydrologists; Industrial Engineers; Industrial Machinery Mechanics; Inspectors, Testers, Sorters, Samplers, and Weighers; Insurance Sales Agents; Interior Designers; Internists; Landscape Architects; Lawyers; Librarians; Licensed Practical and Licensed Vocational Nurses; Loan Officers; Manicurists and Pedicurists; Marriage and Family Therapists; Massage Therapists; Mechanical Engineers; Medical and Health Services Managers; Mixing and Blending Machine Setters, Operators, and Tenders; Nursing Aides, Orderlies, and Attendants; Obstetricians and Gynecologists; Occupational Health and Safety Specialists; Occupational Health and Safety Technicians; Occupational Therapists; Occupational Therapy Assistants; Optometrists; Oral and Maxillofacial Surgeons; Pediatricians; Pesticide Handlers, Sprayers, and Applicators, Vegetation; Pharmacists; Physical Therapist Assistants; Physical Therapists; Physician Assistants; Pipe layers; Plumbers, Pipefitters, and Steamfitters; Podiatrists; Public Relations Specialists; Public Relations and Fundraising Managers; Real Estate Brokers; Real Estate Sales Agents; Recreation Workers; Registered Nurses; Respiratory Therapists; Retail Salespersons; Roofers; Securities, Commodities, and Financial Services Sales Agents; Soil and Plant Scientists; Special Education Teachers; Substance Abuse and Behavioral Disorder Counselors; Supervisors of Construction and Extraction Workers; Surgeons; Surveyors; Ushers, Lobby Attendants, and Ticket Takers; Veterinarians; Veterinary Technologists and Technicians; Vocational Teachers; Water and Wastewater Treatment Plant and System Operators; Welders, Cutters, Solderers, and Brazers... all that matters to the system is that test companies, bureaucrats, and colleges get paid.

If we cannot remove licensure, how can we ensure more people with the temperament, drive, and ability to become a care worker can become one?

We begin by first allowing more people to test into licensure. People learn skills from all over the world and in many ways. Veterans, 'lower-level' workers, and industry workers learn through experience while others who are formerly educated go to great lengths to diversify their education. A student with 200 credits may not hold a degree in a particular field, but that does not mean their education was not in that particular field. Simply, to get a degree, a student must fulfill the core requirements, the department requirements, and (often) the State or agency requirements to confer a degree. All people should be able to prove their knowledge of a subject to be employed in it (if testing is the bar we are requiring as a society).

For instance: A student who holds a degree in biomedical engineering is not educationally qualified to be a Certified Nurse's Assistant (CNA) regardless of the direct care classes he/she took to get their degree. Degrees are limited in their scope to very specific employment opportunities under our licensure structure.

Further, a CNA with 30 years of hands-on experience in emergency rooms and doctor's offices has no right to test into being a nurse. Yet, a 2-year college graduate who has never worked in a hospital (or at any job in their life) is qualified to be a nurse if they have locked in the credentialing classes.

In our system, knowledge and experience should matter. The solution then is simple: allow people to test into licensure. This quick solution will flood the markets with qualified individuals. A market full of workers is a market without rations. Affordable healthcare is an option, we need only allow it.

Your Choice, Your Voice, Our Future - Richard Lee Light

References:

Association of Test Publishers (2017) Questions About Testing in Certification and Licensure Settings; 601 Pennsylvania Ave., N.W. South Building, Suite 900 Washington, DC 20004

Chapter 6
Rehabilitating a Prison System

The need for rehabilitation greatly outweighs the need for incarceration and the resulting, conditioned perpetually violent and or stigmatizing prison incarceration. The benefits of redesign include lowering the burden on the tax payer, offering a future and potential for prosperity to the "criminal", positively increases the ability of the corrections and mental health systems, and societally driving institutionalism toward a better system for all persons.

Research

As prisons fill and addicts litter the prison system, non-violent offenders overcrowd our prisons. There is a distinct battle separating an addict from jails as societally we push for removing things that offend our sensibilities. The result is a prison system that reaps billions in tax payer money while permanently housing and conditioning non-violent offenders to be violent and unable to overcome the stigmas that will follow them through their lives. Addicts and other non-violent offenders indefinitely carry a label of criminal, denying them opportunities for a prosperous future.

The last 20 years have demonstrated volumes of clear understanding as to what corrections and rehabilitation are capable of. Treatment programs aimed at curbing risk, needs, and responsivity have been shown to reduce recidivism (relapsing into criminal behaviour). Further, sanctions (authoritative permission or approval, as for an action; something that serves to support an action, condition; something that gives binding force, as to an oath, rule of conduct;

a provision of a law enacting a penalty for disobedience or a reward for obedience) without rehabilitation are proven ineffective.

The study: *"INTENSIVE REHABILITATION SUPERVISION: THE NEXT GENERATION IN COMMUNITY CORRECTIONS?"* evaluated cognitive-behavioural treatment (CBT) delivered within the context of intensive community supervision via electronic monitoring (EM). Via a scientific control group, researchers are able to eliminate and isolate variables. The aforementioned study statistically matched risks and needs of inmates both in an EM program and those facing only incarceration.

> *"Intensive supervision programs" (ISP's) that have demonstrated reductions in recidivism are those that went beyond simple control and also attempted to provide a significant treatment component (Jolin & Stipak, 1992; Paparozzi & Gendreau, 1993; Pearson, 1988). The most compelling data comes from: The Paparozzi's Bureau of Parole program which deliberately targeted only high risk parolees; across three indices, the recidivism rates for the ISP group were 21-29 percent lower than for a carefully matched sample of regular parolees. Secondly, critiques of the Pearson (1988) study have overlooked the fact that reductions in recidivism were 30 percent lower for those in ISP versus a comparison group in the case of the highest-risk probationers (Gendreau, & Cullen, 1994).*

The results of this study were clear in that "treatment was effective in reducing recidivism for higher risk offenders, confirming the risk principle of offender treatment". There shows a clear need for matching treatment intensity to offender risk and implementing treatment components in intensive supervision programs (such as prison) (Bonta, 2000).

The empirical evidence regarding ISP's is clear: reductions in recidivism are attained with a well implemented Intensive supervision program that targets risks and needs. The obstruction to this reprogramming is political as the for-profit model of corrections empowers legislators and profiteers. The solution lies within communities, non-profits, and local level initiatives.

The Cure

With community driven programs, non-profit entities, and a field of combined counselor/officers, the prison system (and tax payers) can realize major savings in removing non-violent offenders from prison. The opportunities for offenders, high quality officers, and human-services educators are numerous. Society benefits not only from the immediate results upon offenders' lives, but also in the impacts reconditioning deviant behaviours in the institutional cores of the population.

References

Gendreau, P., & Cullen, F. T. (1994). Intensive rehabilitation supervision: The next generation in community corrections? *Federal Probation, 58*(1), 72.

JAMES BONTA (2000) A Quasi-Experimental Evaluation of an Intensive Rehabilitation Supervision Program. *Criminal Justice and Behavior June* 2000 vol. 27 no. 3 312-329

Your Choice, Your Voice, Our Future - Richard Lee Light

Chapter 7

Energy Costs, Production, and Innovation

One of Maine's most pressing economic concerns is energy. We have debates being waged about solar versus gas, whether net metering is good for Mainers, and where the crony dollars for subsidies should go. In the debate about Maine's energy we are often lied to for the monetary benefits of people like Angus King and other benefactors of crony legislation and propaganda.

Maine's Carbon Footprints

Let's begin with some real discussion about why energy is important. Lots of millennials and green-oriented folks support solar and work to put solar on homes as often as possible. We look forward to the day that solar is better than 14% efficient and appreciate a system that can be installed on our homes to diminish the need for foreign oils. While the programming is consistent in these desires, Maine is not the best place for solar. Further, our carbon 'footprint' in Maine is not only one of the lowest in the nation (we are the 3rd cleanest State), but we are one of the greenest states in the world. The catch in our carbon 'footprint' is that it isn't energy production that makes Maine have a carbon footprint... it is cars. Looking to our energy production as a tool for reducing carbon is preposterous and propaganda. Maine cannot get better results through energy production and in fact, anything we add to our system in Maine will decrease our green rating and increase our footprint (including adding solar and wind).

Where we get our Power

Mainers have spent millions of dollars on solar and wind initiatives. As a result Maine has destroyed mountains and mountain ranges in order to make massive windmills. Towns have been destroyed in this process and Maine has lost hundreds of millions of dollars for cronies such as Maine Senator (ex-Governor) Angus King to pocket a fortune. The result is that we have huge machines burning oil to appear green. A windmill uses oil to stay running (which it does when the wind is too weak to turn the windmill); they use oil energy to stay spinning nearly as much as they spin without it. The actual efficiency of windmills is almost inexistent and other States have hundreds of acres of windfarm graveyards to prove this point. Wind is not the technology of green energy, it is the tool for green (cash money) theft. Wind mills are not only inefficient but they often burst into flames from the heat of their oil engines... The result of a windfarm is increased oil use, wonton destruction of Maine's forests (which clean carbon), collapsing local economies (since people get sick from windmills within miles of one), and profit profit profit!

Maine gets some power from solar but the reality of solar is that it is so inefficient and inconsistent that solar causes economic harm to Mainers (we will discuss the power grid further in this chapter). Solar is useful for those with it, but costly for those who do not...

Hydroelectric power is one of the most sustainable and efficient sources of power and yet Maine has made an effort to reduce it. Maine has a lot of water: rivers, streams, and ponds/lakes. Maine has many dams and yet, instead of investing (or even maintaining hydro power), Maine has actively decreased the number of hydroelectric dams.

Lastly, gas and nuclear electricity come to Maine from Canada. The costs for this power are dirt cheap as they are highly efficient (nuclear more so). The issues we have in buying this form of energy is that many Mainers assume it is more beneficial to our nation, our state, and our globe to focus on the creation of green energies rather than purchasing proven resources from Canada.

Your Choice, Your Voice, Our Future - Richard Lee Light

As a result, instead of buying power from the cheapest and most useful energy companies, we rely on the "grid".

Maine loses in order to stay on the grid.

Chapter 8

Fixed income: Retired, Disabled, and robbed.

This chapter is dedicated to reviewing what is it to have your fixed income destroyed by politics and bad economics. Not only is the cost of living for those who paid into and collect social security going down because of mismanagement and government theft of the 'investment' (please review Chapter 2: Fiat Economics and Chapter 9: Maine Based Retirement), but people who worked so hard to prepare for their retirement face depreciation of their money by 12 to 30 percent annually as a result of bailouts, printed money, political games, and private bank control of our government.

Mainers on fixed income face assaults from both sides of the equation as their incomes have less purchasing power and concurrently less cash on hand. The solutions to this are radical, but so too was the idea that social security could exist.

Retired Mainers need a clear picture of why and how their money is diminishing.

Costs

Raising wages, raising gas taxes, raising sales taxes, raising income taxes, raising healthcare costs, and raising educational spending all add to the burden of costs. These inflations (which are shrouded in lies about low pay and poverty) all contribute to higher costs on every purchase.

Raising the minimum wage has no result but needing to zero the balance of labor costs by raising the costs of products. People on fixed income do not get a raise, but for a 17-year-old to have more money for his PlayStation games we raise minimum wage (proposed right now to be doubled from 7.50$ to 15). Whether or not you think low wage, entry level workers should make more money, the reality of the generosity of giving them a 100% income increase means those on fixed income will lose exactly half of their money's value. This is simple math, but this is math which is often not understood or misrepresented. The actual result of doubling the minimum wage is that the prices of all goods and services double. Minimum wage workers have a bigger check but that is a math game which gains them nothing and causes those on fixed incomes to spend exactly twice what they pay now for food, gas, clothes, entertainment...quit literally everything doubles in cost.

Raising gas taxes is a sure-fire way to provide more money to the roads as gas taxes fund these projects. And yet, as much as we tax gas, the result is that our roads are worse, road crews are less productive, costs are ever higher, and crony politicians and gravel & tar corporations reap millions in excessive profits. Gas companies make 9 cents per gallon (and people bemoan the billions in profit these corporations make) while the government makes 43 cents per gallon (5 times as much money as oil companies...). Gas taxes increasing means people on fixed income spend more to go the same distances. This tax takes grandparents from their grandkids as costs to travel become too high to make trips out.

Raising sales tax is a favoured game of politicians. This is a tax that costs pennies per product and doesn't add up to a noticeable pain until we go shopping for food, cars, go to a movie, or make another purchase more than a few dollars. This method of taxation is impossible to fight, curb, control, or have representation for. We as Americans are supposed to be able to have representation for our taxes (that is to say we have the right to determine where our money goes). Sales taxes have no method of representation; they are put forth by computer and bleed people slowly. No one is more affected by sales tax increases than those on fixed income.

Raising income taxes seems like a tax that would not affect those on fixed income. The truth is that as wages are increased, taxes are increased. Just like they say to shave your face when you get a new haircut, lawmakers attempt to hide their tax increases inside the raising of minimum wage. This form of deception works. Workers who make X$ per week still make more money, yet the government makes double their prior money off those increased checks AND gain some added money from their increased percentages. The worker ends up paying more than double the amount of taxes while the person on fixed income covers all the costs through raising prices on purchases. There is no tax which doesn't pinch and harm those on fixed income.

Raising healthcare and education spending destroys the incomes of those on fixed income. The best way to make people look evil is by using kids, the sick, and the elderly as purported victims. We spend more on education and healthcare than any nation in the world. As a result, we have the worst educational and healthcare systems of first-world nations. The trillions of dollars in healthcare and educational spending Americans are taxed for do NOT go to teachers, doctors, nurses, counselors, nor the students, nor the patients. Our tax money instead goes, first to corporate entities that control government ensured monopolies, and then to the government cronies who helped assure these contracts. Politicians and lobbyists steal money from this pool before handing the funds to unions and administrators. These unions and administrators steal nearly half of the money (note my rebudget 2016 for sourcing) before finally paying the people who do the work, teach the kids, test and experiment with innovations, and work to help people. The result on the dollar of those on fixed income is that property taxes skyrocket; renters and home owners alike pay for these increases.

Increased costs destroy the purchasing power of those on fixed incomes. Raises for fixed income do not match GDP nor do they match inflation. Raises for fixed incomes are a product of politicians looking for votes.

Your Choice, Your Voice, Our Future - Richard Lee Light

Cost of living increases:

January 2006 -- 4.1%

January 2007 -- 3.3%

January 2008 -- 2.3%

January 2009 -- 5.8%

January 2010 -- 0.0%

January 2011 -- 0.0%

January 2012 -- 3.6%

January 2013 -- 1.7%

January 2014 -- 1.5%

January 2015 -- 1.7%

January 2016 -- 0.0%

Source: https://www.ssa.gov/news/cola/automatic-cola.htm

A President's first year in office sets the tone for how they are received throughout their tenure. Barack Obama is noted in the above chart but all presidents and elected officials play this game. Notice that the "Economic stimulus package" of 2008 by Bush was used as a tool for gaining Republican support in the 2008 election. In 2009 Obama pushed through a raise for social security. His generosity stopped for the two years of his first presidency (no increase at all) until his re-election in 2012 where the Democrats tried to buy support by raising the COLA (5.8%). A steady gain had been offered to seniors for three years and is now at zero again as we head for a new election. You can be guaranteed that there will be a COLA increase either just before the election of 2016 or just after a new president takes office. If a Republican looks poised to win, A proposed raise will come before November; if a Democrat looks poised to win, they will reward their victory with a minor increase on their first year in office. Either way, your investment is being used against you to gather favour in political games.

The real disservice here is this: if this chart of "cost of living" increases was an investment account, the company offering these gains annually would be put out of business. Social security was not only robbed long ago by politicians paying for more wars, more programs, and more profits in corporate pockets, but it is so far below the return of an investment account that is should be criminal.

If you paid into social security, you were not only robbed of your ability to choose how it is invested, but you have been robbed every day since. This money should have been invested by people who know how to make money, not by those who steal money. Retirement accounts all over the world would have generated, and would continue to generate, 10% (and more) interest while the United States Federal Government offers mostly 1% and often 0%.

You deserve more for your work and your money should grow your future, not line the pockets of government thieves.

What can we do?

The solutions to this issue are as radical as the idea of social security. This money needs to leave the United States central government piggy bank and be placed in an account closer to home. Like any 401k or other retirement investment program, every dollar of your money needs to be placed in multiple portfolios and invested by professionals. Any losses generated by an investor can be partially recovered and with this process of the market liability can be prosecuted. When the government loses or steals money you lose the money and NO ONE suffers a day in jail

Your Choice, Your Voice, Our Future - Richard Lee Light

or even a lost job. Instead, the government dumps dollar after dollar into their pocket and you get nothing.

Diversification is the key here and investors know how to make more money than they lose. And, if you worry about this process because you feel there may be more losses than gains (risk), we can compare the federal social security program with the Maine retirement program. While 2.1% is a moderate gain, the stable 2.1% blows away the earnings gains of the federal social security program.

Ultimately, we have three options:

1. We can leave the money where it is and lose any solvency, allow corrupt D.C politicians to rob the funds, and watch as the debt clock spools higher to replace the losses.
2. We can sue the federal government as a State for the earnings of Mainers within their pool of our cash and then use this money to invest as a State or in private investment programs (See Chapter 9: Maine Based Retirement)
3. Or, we can use a hybrid system where we put new money (of current workers) into a State based or private based retirement system while letting the money the federal government governs continue its path with those who currently collect.

Further Considerations

The USD will continue to depreciate; It can be expected that the decrease in value will be in the 20% to 30% range.

(http://philosophyofmetrics.com/us-dollar-will-devalue-by-20-to-30-freepom/)

Fixed-income investors are the hardest hit by inflation. Suppose that a year ago, you invested $1,000 in a Treasury bill with a 10% yield. Now that you are about to collect the $1,100 owed to you, is your $100 (10%) return real? Of course not! Assuming inflation was positive for the year, your purchasing power has fallen and, therefore, so has your real return. We should consider the chunk inflation has taken out of your return. If inflation was 4%, then your return is really 6%.

This example highlights the difference between "nominal interest rates" and "real interest rates". The nominal interest rate is the growth rate of your money, while the real interest rate is the growth of your purchasing power. In other words, the real rate of interest is the nominal rate reduced by the rate of inflation. In our example, the nominal rate is 10% and the real rate is 6% (10% - 4% = 6%).

(http://www.investopedia.com/university/inflation/inflation4.asp#ixzz47PTJWVba)

Your Choice, Your Voice, Our Future - Richard Lee Light

Chapter 9
Maine Based Retirement?

This is less of a plan and more of an innovative dialog. There is no future in Social Security (reference Chapter 2: 'Fiat Economics: Potato Economics") and we need to act soon for our kids, our workers, our selves, and our State but the solutions would be not only difficult to implement, they could spark a war between the bank-owned central government and individuals who wish not to be owned by a private, global banking monarch. This concept of a State-based retirement program is not the most individual-centric version of a retirement program, but, it is considerably more individual-centric than the federal Social Security Program. As with all government programs: the more local the control, the more individualistically controlled it is.

Considerable Data

Maine State employees (Maine bureaucrats) consist of teachers, corrections officers, mental health workers, road workers, bridge crews, DMV workers, DOJ staff, DOE Administrators, Legislators, State-House workers, Accountants, Lawyers, Doctors, Police officers, Fire Fighters, Park Rangers, Wardens, and many, many more...

Every Bureaucrat works for tax dollars. These tax dollars are taxed by the State (a game of shells where fake money floods the system of tax money creating a phony accounting scheme by which government can spend more than they take in). This tax money comes to Bureaucrats in the form of pay (76% above the same jobs in the private sector), School Loan repayment (upwards of 138,000$ for many recipients), Continued Education (3,000 to 60,000 dollars per year),

Healthcare (fully paid family plans), Dental care (partially paid and often fully paid family plans), Family benefits for education and student loan repayment, and a Retirement package which pays 75-80% of the income of a bureaucrats' top-paid 3 years of State employment. Realistically, Maine has a platinum employment system. The caveat is that the best employment, at the best pay, with the best benefits in Maine is as a State employee being paid by the tax payers of Maine.

Focusing on the retirement program run by MainePERS in Augusta, we can see that a Maine-based retirement program is not only possible, but is in effect and posting gains as a retirement program. Retirees of the Maine State bureaucracy are paid consistently and with Cost-of-Living increases which average 2.2%. Compared to the Unites States' Social Security program, the Maine State retirement program averages a better interest rate and is actually solvent (the Social Security program has been robbed by politicians and is in debt; money paid into social security today is not enough to pay for the money being paid-out, let alone having funds for investment). The United States' Social Security program is not sustainable; anyone under 50 should understand by now that Social Security will not be there for our retirement. We need to rethink retirement and for us to have anything in our senior years, everyone under 50 needs a new option. I propose a State option.

Having a State-based retirement program is simple to implement. The system is already in place for moving money from incomes into a retirement program; all we need to do is redirect the federal social security theft from our pay checks into a Maine-Based retirement program. The benefits of this program are numerous. This program will benefit tax-payers (as it has bureaucrats) in several ways.

1) Maine's retirees will see more money in their retirement checks; this has been realized already in comparing MainePERS' pay-outs for retirees to those of Social Security recipients.

Your Choice, Your Voice, Our Future - Richard Lee Light

2) Maine workers who are taxed for social security will not be wasting their money on a system which has proven to be insolvent, stolen from, and ineffective.

3) Mainers who will not be able to collect Social Security when the social security account officially collapses (predicted for anyone under 50) will have a system of retirement such as has benefited our parents, grandparents, and great grandparents.

4) Employees in bureaucratic State employment will be able to change jobs from department to department or from public to private employment and continue their accrual of retirement funds.

    a. Employees who are burned-out in corrections, mental health, physically stressful jobs, or in any other capacity within State Employment can easily change jobs. This will better tend to the capacity and ability of bureaucrats who are unable or unwilling to perform their duties but retain their employment when they are simply there to "Get their retirement"

    b. The societal impacts are endless when we can ensure bureaucrats who are unable or unwilling to perform their duties to Maine with quality and compassion are able and encouraged to seek employment which better suits their abilities, temperament, and passions.

5) Maine's economy will be drastically impacted as we stop paying for bureaucratic contributions to Social Security (which they often do not receive; also known as "double-dipping").

6) Mainers will realize a fairer system of retirement where bureaucrats do not utilize tax money to receive a greater retirement benefit than those who worked to generate the taxes. All retirees will be able to benefit from a fairer system.

7) The effectiveness of retirement accounts is greatest when the investor can not only track their investment, but can access the agency which manages their accounts. Being able to have a voice and influence over retirement is something the federal government is unable to offer in any 'service' it provides. Control is only available in this nation at the most local level (in this event, the local level is Augusta not the endless bureaucracies of Washington D.C.)

There is NO reason Maine cannot begin and maintain a retirement program. The battle for this begins in the knowledge of the inability and dead-end of the federal Social Security Program, the understanding that this system does not benefit everyone, the wisdom to understand that our current system is unfair and benefits only the Bureaucracy at the cost of private sector employees, a will to want a better retirement system, the fact that we have the tools in Maine already to implement this, the desire to want a better system for our kids and workers, and the voice of an educated and well-thinking, well-meaning people to tell our government to do better for the people.

Reference:

http://www.mainepers.org/Pensions/NPP_Report_3-5-2012.pdf

Chapter 10
The Forest for The Trees

The consistent and repeated theme throughout the strategies provided in this book have been reducing government control and thus allowing the economy to once again grow. Regardless of the numbers, the references, and the real-life experiences of readers, there will be quite a few who are conditioned into subservience to the system. These folks will never, regardless of the logic, facts, and history, be able to see government as anything but a benevolent entity. This battle is one fought in the deepest recesses of the programmed minds of Americans.

The ways in which reducing the government's control over markets can and will benefit our economy and our futures are many. In reducing government control, we will increase the paychecks of workers, create more jobs, provide better conditions for workers, ensure that we are legally protected from abuse, and increase the opportunities for a prosperous and free life.

Government Control Destroys Workers' Futures

Every minute you work is not paid. More than 30% of most people's paychecks are stolen for redistribution. The goal of redistribution is to pool capitalism's excesses (some of the profits of capitalism) into a community pool used for advancing our common goods and ensuring a safety net for those who fall on hardship or are unable to maintain a minimum existence. The reality of redistribution is that money is stolen from workers to pay for bureaucrats and corporate sponsorship. Worker's money is not given to people in need (some is, and this small percentage is used to propagate the need for government redistribution) as much as it is given to contractors, politicians' buddies and families, and taken as paychecks from bureaucrats.

Redistribution

Corporate bailouts and subsidies are given as payoffs for major contributions to campaigns. In this way, politicians take tens of thousands of dollars from corporate sponsors and return the favor by promoting legislation that redirects millions of tax dollars into the pockets of their sponsors. The list of crony tax-theft is evident on all sides of the aisle, and regardless of what the media tells you, this theft is equally prevalent in both "parties". Campaign contributions and the resulting crony legislation is difficult to track but it is being tracked. Find a watchdog entity and follow the money... but, do not expect others to follow or care. To the many Americans blinded by dissonance, the idea of crony politicians and corporations (crony-corporatism) is a conspiracy theory and evidence of it is just "fake-news". This is an uphill battle.

Bonds

Bonds are another political game. A bond is a loan. Communities and States are often barraged with new bond requests for schools, roads, conservation, and whatever other emotional trigger-words the writers can think of (kids, elderly, poor, etc.). The reality is that most of the money of a bond will find the pockets of crony contractors and other special interests with their hands in the pockets of the politicians who are charged with delivering the bond money to a service provider. Beyond the initial theft of this money into the greedy pockets of corporate and crony interest is the accrued interest on the money. Out taxes are being stolen in advance through bonds.

Your Choice, Your Voice, Our Future - Richard Lee Light

We are spending money on pet projects and crony contractors that we have not yet earned. When your town takes out a loan (bond), your property tax is being increased, when the State takes out a loan (bond), your property tax, sales tax, and income tax increases. Now, to a renter with no job the idea that property tax and income tax are acceptable to be extorted is common; it is again up to the public to make their case against extortion in lieu of those proponents who have no 'skin in the game'.

Bureaucracy

The largest setback in prosperity is bureaucracy. Government workers receive most of the money we spend in taxes. Government workers are not only paid better than the workers who generate their government paycheck (76% better), but these bureaucrats also have dental-care, healthcare, childcare, college, gas, homes, cars, and retirement all paid for out of tax money. Workers in the private sector (workers ranging from minimum wage fast food workers to corporate CEOs are paying for bureaucrats to live like kings and retire well-paid, well cared for, and well more prosperous than the tax-payer. While tax payers struggle to meet housing, food, healthcare, dental, educational, and retirement goals (now working into their 70s to survive), bureaucrats are retiring at 38 with a retirement check and full benefits (a package worth more than twice what the worker makes while they grind as slaves into their late life (often dying at work).

Bureaucracy is more destructive than just the money as well. Every job a bureaucrat does is one or more jobs which are taken out of the private sector. We elect people to legislate (create and enforce laws). The electorate has installed bureaucrats to help them achieve their goals in legislation. This process would be fine if it were the legislator using their money (which tax payers pay them) to hire helpers. The reality is however that the legislators hire a group of people with more tax dollars, and then when the elected individual leaves office, their hired staff stay in their new well-tax-paid job while the new legislator hires some more workers to help them with their new laws. This cycle leaves us with a bloated government full of people hired by elected folks who cannot be removed until they retire (on tax money).

Bureaucracy serves no purpose which cannot be outsourced by private entities. While there is a debate on what services should be private and which should be public, there is no question about the need to reduce bureaucracy. Police and fire services are two of the first public services brought up when discussing privatization, and while there is a healthy debate on even privatizing these services (consider: The Police State, Private Property; 07/11/2016 by Murray N. Rothbard), we are too easily distracted from considering other departments and positions as needing to be privatized. The State hires accountants, auditors, inspectors, janitors, road crews, and hundreds of other workers for services that the private sector can and should be doing. By moving the work to the private sector, we return tax producing jobs to the economy rather than providing lucrative tax-paid jobs.

More than the immediate costs of bureaucrats, is how dangerous bureaucrats are. In jobs which the State provides workers, those workers are immune to liability. Most people do not conceive this concept as it seems Ludacris! But, consider what a government is: Government is an entity which can perform atrocities for the people so what no one is liable for the damages or immorality of that action. In other words, government is an entity which can kill, steal, and otherwise harm people in the name of the people and be immune to the judgements which would normally follow those actions. If you were to go to Pakistan and shoot someone, you would be a murderer and would be subject to rule of law. The United States' government on the other hand uses drones, missiles, and soldiers to murder not only insurgents, but innocent women and children. The result is that the United States government is considered an entity beyond legal or

Your Choice, Your Voice, Our Future - Richard Lee Light

moral reproach and is thus immune to prosecution. Similarly, police, corrections officers, drug agents, the FBI, CIA, NSA, and even the EPA kill and steal from citizens without liability. Every agent of the government is protected by the government, leaving them immune to prosecutions and punishment (in more than 99% of cases).

Being immune to liability is dangerous. The EPA can take your land and prosecute you (which it has on many occasions) for building a woodshed too close to a pond (your own pond), the NSA makes it a regular duty to not only monitor, but record your phone calls, emails, and shopping activities (credit card purchases) which it reads and shares freely, and the FBI and CIA regularly (disregarding our rights) invade homes and kill Americans without batting an eye. When we add this lack of liability to jobs like accountants and auditors, mental health workers, and schools we can easily see that being immune to prosecution for theft, abuse, or murder is dangerous for us and our children.

Bureaucracy is the most dangerous and disenfranchising aspect of our government. Bureaucracy needs to be reduced for a better economy, a more equitable society, and a safer existence.

Chapter Last

Your Choice, Your Voice, Our Future

What I am offering Maine is nothing like what others who have run for this position have offered. I have never wanted someone to be my voice, and I do not offer to be yours; only I know what is in my heart as only you know what is in yours. I am using this opportunity to shine light on the system that creates a stage for elites and keeps everyone else from having a voice. I am running for Governor of Maine to educate, and if we win, I am smashing the stage so everyone may have their voice heard equally.

Our system is disenfranchising, falsely binary, oppressive, and fraught with contention and slavery. We can rise against this or we can continue on the same path. It has been the result of the American system that generation after generation left this nation (and the world) freer and more prosperous than the last. We cast off race-based slavery, we have destroyed the notion that one gender should rule while the other obeys, we had built a nation of rights and freedom... but, we have backslidden.

Our nation is not better off than it was a generation ago. We are in unprecedented debt, have resurfaced racism and sexism, we have instilled a class warfare, and we are being oppressed by fascism and authoritarians. Generation X and Millennials have less opportunity, less ability to grow and flourish, and less unity than our grandparents. We have been slowly taken over by a rotting infestation of cronies, puppet masters, propogandists, and dictators. As our nations becomes more centralized, Maine can stand in opposition. We have an opportunity to demonstrate what America has lost.

Your Choice, Your Voice, Our Future - Richard Lee Light

Maine has strong educators, doctors, nurses, social workers, counselors, laborers of all types, and most respectably, we have strong work and moral ethics. Our State has diversity and a will to surpass obstacles and be reveled across the nation and world. We need the will to see an opportunity through the despair. By continuing what we do best, by growing rather than contracting, by embracing innovation and adaptation rather than antiquity and failed ideas, we can guide America back to prosperity. Maine can be the economic engine of tomorrow's America.

Through this book, we have covered Education, Healthcare, ideological spectrums, Corrections, Rehabilitation, Culture, Community, politics, Economics, Energy, business, debt, governance, and a slew of other topics. Through this journey, we have delved into what keeps us from growth, how we can overcome oppressing obstruction, and what we could do to drop the shackles and pick up prosperous freedom.

Reaching a better future for everyone takes change. Change is not always easy; change is often coupled with fear. We need not fear the future and change when we can be so positively impacted. When we decide to swallow our fear and move toward a better future, we will be unstoppable.

I am applying for a job: the executive position of our State of Maine.

This is your choice, your voice, our future.

Thank you,
Richard Light

www.Light4ME.org
#Light4ME2018
#MaineGovernor